T0198998

Portrait of Health presents

A Family That Grows Together

Natiya Guin, ND, MEd
Bobby Buoncristiano, CPT
and our children: Kai, Grace, and Trajan Buoncristiano

Illustrated by: Schenker De Leon
Additional illustrations: Kai, Grace, and Trajan Buoncristiano

Balboa Press books may be ordered through booksellers or by contacting:

Balboa Press
A Division of Hay House
1663 Liberty Drive
Bloomington, IN 47403
www.balboapress.com
1 (877) 407-4847

Because of the dynamic nature of the Internet, any web addresses or links contained in this book may have changed since publication and may no longer be valid. The views expressed in this work are solely those of the author and do not necessarily reflect the views of the publisher, and the publisher hereby disclaims any responsibility for them.

Any people depicted in stock imagery provided by Thinkstock are models, and such images are being used for illustrative purposes only.
Certain stock imagery © Thinkstock.

ISBN: 978-1-5043-8998-3 (sc)
ISBN: 978-1-5043-8999-0 (e)

Library of Congress Control Number: 2017916057

Print information available on the last page.

Balboa Press rev. date: 09/29/2018

BALBOA
PRESS
A DIVISION OF HAY HOUSE

Dedicated to our grandmothers...

Mau Mau for reminding us to stop and smell the roses.

GGLoie for always looking on the bright side.

Mimi for dancing through life.

Inabel for inspiring this book with her love.

Mom-Mom for teaching us to be patient, and trust that what we give, we will eventually get back.

A family that grows together, creates a garden of love.

We begin by growing a row of PEAS,
bringing PEACE to those we meet.

Create your own symbol of peace…

We then grow CARAWAY HERBS, so we always get CARRIED AWAY by JOY.

Next, we add BABY'S BREATH, to remind us to
see the world through the eyes of a CHILD.

10

And we leave only footprints…paint yours.

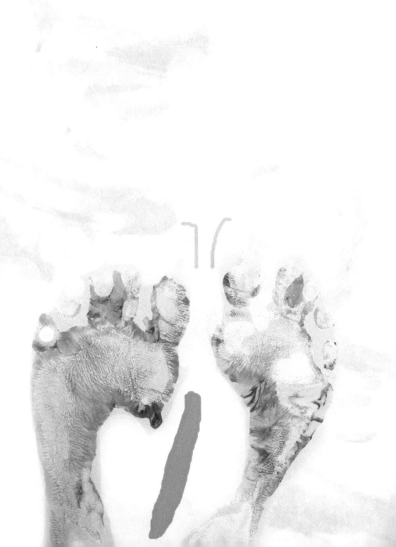

Our parents teach us to grow TURNIPS,

12

because they TURN UP when needed.

Our friends grow FREESIA,
reminding us to live life FREELY.

Draw you and your best friend
making your silliest faces…

Our Grandparents grow MARIGOLDS,
so we remember to always be MERRY and BRIGHT.

We grow SQUASH,
to SQUASH any
self doubt.

We grow FORGET ME NOTS, to remember
how lucky we are to have each other.

Then we add BUTTERCUPS and PUMPKINS, so we always speak to one another with kindness.

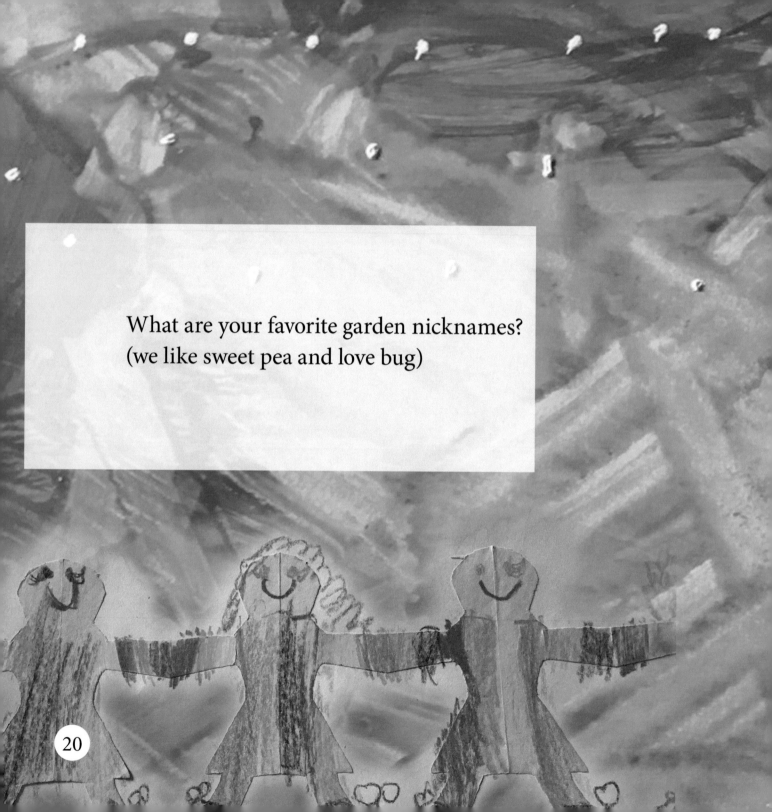

What are your favorite garden nicknames?
(we like sweet pea and love bug)

We grow BIRD OF PARADISE,
may we always keep dreaming.
Draw your perfect PARADISE…

21

We grow ORCHIDS,
so we remain KIDS at heart.

Never forget to
plant SUN FLOWERS,
so you always stand
TALL and PROUD.

Now pick all your favorite veggies and fruits
when they are ripe and ready.

...and make a colorful plate to eat
after a long day of gardening!

A family that GROWS TOGETHER, STAYS TOGETHER.

Printed in the United States
By Bookmasters